In poem after stunning poem, Madelyn Garner's
Hum of Our Blood elegizes the son she knew and
loved in all his human dimensions, speaking into
those spaces usually left silent between mothers
and sons. In a book of truth and life as much as it
is about AIDS and death, Garner sheds lights both
warm and bright on the darkest corners of gay
existence in the 1980s and '90s from a perspective
continually surprising and, as strange as it may
seem, delightful.

— Michael Broder, *Drug and Disease Free*

— Jason Schneiderman, *Primary Source*

HUM OF OUR BLOOD

HUM OF OUR BLOOD

Poems

MADELYN GARNER

ʒ

THREE: A TAOS PRESS

Book Design: Michele Braverman, BraveStudio, Inc., Denver, CO
Cover and Interior Photographs: Bradley Joseph Braverman
Front Cover Model: Pineniece Joshua
Press Logo Design: William Watson, Castro Watson, New York, NY
Text Typeset in Tisa Pro

Printed in the United States of America by Cottrell Printing Company

ISBN: 978-0-9972011-5-4

THREE: A TAOS PRESS
P.O. Box 370627
Denver, CO 80237
www.3taospress.com

10 9 8 7 6 5 4 3 2 1

In Memory of Bradley Joseph Braverman

17 February 1961 – 10 January 1996

Contents

HUM OF OUR BLOOD

At the Beginning

This was L A where they touched over and over,

kissed each other on the mouth,

danced like brides until mirrors swallowed them,
    spit them out

     bone

skin a shrink-wrap
translucence.

•

Did we hear their every word over the orgy of dinner dishes?

*my tongue feels like flannel / watch out for sarcoma's hard-fist / I'm tired
of keeping track of viral loads / their irrational numbers / no, Troy hasn't
yet licked the monkey... .*

•

Where was a Louis Pasteur
with a glass-necked swan, bag of pipettes, ethanol beaker?

An effective vaccination?

A miracle?

•

Ambulance drivers refused to come.
Doctors said, lethal.

Even in death, they were lepers.

Bodies cocooned in black plastic and taped
for crematoriums, left outside
hospital walls like garbage.

•

Warning:

> If the mouth sours, don't spit.
> If salt-lipped, don't drink from the same glass.
> If skin peels even the thinnest layer, don't leak anything thicker than pitch.
> If struck or torn or bitten, don't bleed.
> If the thigh is touched, don't breathe.

•

Tsunami's vast changes to the bodyscape:

> trembling and wreckage
>
> unsafe shores
>
> whole cities sinking.

So many dying.
All the ways they were dying.
The reason they were.

Plenty

The early years when he lives simply by his fingertips—
     driving along California's cultivated fields
     before pulling over to gather sunflowers
     one fistful after another.

     Eating Chinese takeout, trading graphic
     designs for a good set of tires.

It is also the years of the lens—
     shooting commercials of androgynous models,
     their frozen eyes, pursed lips that pay the rent.

     Blank canvases into which he falls
     headlong: his hand tracing the smell of hair,
     skin's atonal notes.

It is days, too, of restless assemblage as desire—
     scavenging thrift and secondhand stores, Watts
     to Beverly Hills, for objets d'art—
     for cuffed shirts of Egyptian cotton and white as
     Calla lilies.

Or day for night in which he considers
     the promise of infinite variations
     in his rummage for skin—
     where there are never enough Eves
     to his Adam.

Drum

The day we linked arms on the terrace of the Getty Villa,
dizzy from art and wine and the view
overlooking Malibu, cascades of bougainvillea,

unaware that if he were celibate, he might live.
If I were Pharaoh's daughter,
I would free him from the hungry rushes of the Nile.

He pretended to embrace a marble figure so radiant
it might have been sculpted by Praxiteles himself—
the pool's reflecting transcendence.

Why didn't the angel come at that moment
of sun on our skin, hum of our blood,
when his heart was beating its four-chambered drum?

Body Studies in Black and White

Because his camera is enraptured
by the unclothed world, it speaks in tongues
of the body, flesh and breath,

as it captures the shimmer of sweat
under klieg lights; the way a simple touch
triggers trembling. Close-ups

not of Venus rising, but Mound of Venus;
not pistil, but phallus; not fin,
but submerged arms reaching upward in radiance.

Sex is only part of it as the camera praises
the beauty of hair's texture, braided/unbraided,
short or long, falling as veil or shawl,

baldness as sculpture. Meditations
on the mysteries of an ankle; spine as filigree,
fuse, or furrow; revelation

of hips as hills. Nipples like common cosmos in bloom.
And O! the breast. Eyes, kohl-lined or nude;
mouth—its ecstasies, its stories.

These Hallelujahs.

Another Gay Mugging

He walks
out the door of his third-floor Silver Lake studio

past concrete walls color-walloped with piss and graffiti

through the fog of vented steam and its sibilant hiss
pocket of greasy heat between dumpsters
hard-slung curses in the air

dangers the ear's inlet and canals
do not recognize

before the neighborhood crew
their skin corrupted by numerology and *fuck off*

flush my son out

smash his face with fists and steel-toed boots
leaving death's bloody print on him
as if to eliminate the flaw

in him? in them?

Neighbors deafened by television's waves upon
waves of gleaming appliances and
spinning wheels

hear nothing

not his cries
not the dark rumors of red froth
not his bones stunned and buckling.

The Baths, 1982

Virus HTLV arrives disguised as hunger
in the beautiful bodies slamming

against each other—water serpenting over hip bones,
along groins to patches of thatch; eager

mouths French kissing nipples
into glistening pearls; possessed cocks,

engorged and driven like pistons, exploding
in each pink-cheeked Mozart—creator

of complex études for four hands.
Each of them hot:

the married man, whip in his jocks (touch me here);
rent-boys with pockets stuffed full

of condoms   (and here); tourists
mapping a new geography   (yes, here and here);

Father Tim who pads around naked
and hard, just like our sons on the threshold

of coming out and eager.
Tattooed on the shoulder of mine—

How many times can I be kissed before I die?

His First Symptom

Taste of dime on the tongue.

More signs come: green-tinged clouds lining the horizon, a brisk wind finger-spelling rain on a cheek. In the elms, crows as Greek chorus begin their lament.

If there is pain, it is a gust snapping the corners of curtains before billowing outward.

A door blown shut.

Sometimes it is blood at morning. Which is foreboding. Which is fear as flesh pockets grow heavy with expectation, stone and stone. Trees with skeletal fingers. A rumbling overhead.

Triptych: Days of Diagnosis

As Ouija Board

These days his appointments
are séances:

body wrapped in white paper
under unbearable lights
laid out flat as the board.

He watches the doctor's fingers move
over the cadence of his chest, moat
of his belly,

as if listening to ghost whispers
from the spirit world spelling out

one letter at a time

the possible reasons
things are out-of-rhythm.

Still, to each question he answers
yes or no, *(sometimes maybe)*,
fearing for the future

every time the heart-shaped planchette,
shivering against shivering,
points to *carnage.*

As Etch-A-Sketch

When he shakes the box

aluminum dust swallows
the gray lines of his gaunt face—

once full lips now thinned to slash,
bleak eyes—
their icy weather.

Blank slate

ready for thumb and finger
to grasp white knobs,
coax the metal stylus to create

a line for cheek,
once youthful brow, glinting like mica.

No matter
how many versions he erases,

his hand outlines from the half-light
of particles the same face,

the same spot of Kaposi's sarcoma
on the chin—

silver stigmata
colder than moonstone.

As Playground Swing

Some moments, it is about ascent—his eyes on vapor trails like white
threads seaming a sky so blue it could be untrue.

Feet out in front, toes pointed toward the place above the canopy of trees
he reaches for apex. Moment between rise and fall when he feels
weightless—free—beyond today's terror of what his blood tests will show.

Still fixable.

Other moments? It is about gravity, pull of the earth.

About falling. Air a hand pressed against his neck. Stomach heaving
fear or reflex. Pitch and roll of the planet. Then, dragging his heels
in the ground, the jerk of chains. The shudder.

MADELYN GARNER

When He Tells

The wine seems unusually red   the salad more bitter   the meat seeps   blood
floods the vegetables   his hands shake throughout the meal as if he hears
footsteps   he knows I won't weep or fall to the floor because we are in a restaurant
(his plan)   he kisses my cheek   says he will see me in the morning   he is
leaving   I see an approaching camel bearing shrouds and sack cloth   night falls
and falls   winter's dark weather is colder.

MADELYN GARNER

After Braverman's Suicide Suite, Gallery Show, Los Angeles, 1994

The jarring images will shock,
but seem entirely appropriate to the theme
of life as a tightrope to walk on or hang by.
                                    —Los Angeles Reader

Brad asks his HIV-positive friends
how they might choose
to take their lives instead of shriveling
into body bags of skin.

One selects his apartment's gas stove,
lying down on a checkerboard
floor, holding his breath at each click
of the aperture as if inhaling
the sweet scent of the Stargazer lilies
he says counterbalance
the sweat-filled night. Another

sits in his classic convertible,
arranges the muzzle of a gun
with experienced fingers,
his famous face hidden
by the splatter of Eucalyptus shadows.

Tony and Bill can't decide. Lovers' Leap?
Cocktails spiked with arsenic? Then—
Tony decides death from hanging,

his feet divining for gravity, and
Bill settles for a cinder-block-weighted
fall into his favorite Palm Springs pool.

Shane selects plastic, sticky
and tightly wrapped. Cadaver air
stinging his nose as he tries to lie
still in a rumpled bed,
surrounded by swollen pillows,
creased sheets, listening to *love, love you baby.*

In the last photo session, Brad leans
into the lens to capture his newest love
on a sandy patch of beach pliant
as skin, wondering how many more times
will they be pulled by
desire's gravitational tides.

During the year it takes him to print
these portraits—he tries tricking
his body with black market cures, building
muscle mass in Gold's Gym and
acting out noir fantasies at a crowded
club named Cuffs.

In the end, he sets the shutter speed on infinity.
Let death come.

The Years Between

He hears the virus multiplying   weevils skittering along arteries, burrowing in
cells the flour of skin   knows that some of his friends, invaded by mandibles, pack
their throats with dirt   coin their eyes   others slip away almost easily   fingers
light on the rope of capsized lifeboats   but every day he blends exotic botanicals into
fluorescent shakes   transforms the enema into ritual   tries ice/fire/bleach   stands
dizzy with fever in the long line at the free clinic for a biochemical fix   consumed
by hope that this time his numbered syringe   will be the singular needle in
the haystack.

The Clinic Calls To Say

Another missed appointment
in that place where wall clocks
pocket minutes,

and every sip from the fountain
tastes of tin.

He claims he was there, fever-tethered
to a utilitarian chair
even as the hallways emptied,

listening not for his name but a number.

I want him to have a simple explanation,

but he withdraws the tail end
of a worn lottery ticket

from his left-hand jacket pocket, stuck
within a wad of Kleenex, stick
of stale gum.

First evidence his brain is shriveling:
no numbers on which to hook meaning—

in columns or rows,
Roman, bar code, binary—
not even the five fingers he counted on
as a child.

Triptych: Searching for a Cure

As War

What he needs is something more than a handful of GI Joes on offense.

What he needs is Agent Orange sprayed over every branch,
the gradual deforesting of his cells until he is breastplate and bone.

Or napalm—gasoline-fueled gel rippling across skin.

Mushroom cloud scouring him as if he were Hiroshima,
alive and radiant under windless skies—

survivor's glow to his face.

As Side Effect

Yet again a temperature.
Some days soft plumes seeping
into crevices, faint flushing of the face;

other times rabid flash fire
reminding him of the time he stole
a fiercely desired box

of red-tipped matches to light
freeze-dried leaves nested
behind the house:

the unexpected flash, stippling
of blisters, the burn.
Now thirty-four, my son hears

the crackle of kindling
inside his lungs. Coughs. Spits char.
His bones smolder

to marrow, skin-wet stink
of creosote and sulphur,
once beautiful body—molten.

As Last Resort

In the Herbaría, its windows humid green—homeopathic remedies
Gossypol and curcumin and boxwood
The hard bark harvested from the neem tree known as a cure-all
My son's quandary: which roots and berries to eat—which to pass over

The now abandoned medical dictionary he used as decoder ring
Seduction of pill bottles, scree-edged spoon, glass vials
Chemical stew of the medicine cabinet
Astringent smells, hint of bleach, white-tiled rooms

Instead, droppers full of inflorescent tinctures that numb the tongue
Blended shakes taking on the colors of ancient saris
Bundle of sage, silver smoke smudging rooms, and lavender candles
Also, cups of buckthorn tea, orange blossom honey

The ringing of meditation bells / Lotus pose / needles adrift on his skin
Everything he tries to keep the body from turning to stone.

First Person in the World

Lucky day—
HIV positive, then spontaneously negative,

what else could Ray do but offer up
his gleaming blood as a cure

to the world?

Not a week without a band squeezing
his muscular arm, needle

stick, the slow-motion flow
that fills labeled vials, glass silos

waiting in antiseptic rows.

For months scientists sleuth his preferences,
his starry chemistry,

root and stem of his genealogy.
Then day of the sucker punch—

dreaded holocaustian string of numbers

slamming him back
into the land of antiretroviral acronyms:

ABC / 3TC / AZT
that spell terminal.

Under Exhausted Stars

Along the low buildings of the boulevards
and the melting rooftops and the traffic jams,
whispers whirl around this single question:
Where have the despairing gone?

•

Disappeared   as in
exposed, excluded, excoriated, exiled, X'ed-out—
so many words
for one repetitive note of a locked groove,
needle stuck on *fear.*

•

Over months, LA's newspapers track the annihilation by
marquees darkened / blank canvases longing for color /
pairs of ballet tights draped over rehearsal bars / stringless guitars.

•

With certain tenderness, my son
erases smoke from his shirt sleeves
erases time between funerals
erases every trace of the dead from appointment books.

•

I hear my son voice his despair:
They are.
They are not.

The Last Birthday Gift

He rises from the bronze brocade settee,
back to the California sun, Zulu tall, skin wafer thin,

bones carved into ancient mah-jongg tiles
that click as he makes his way to the gold leaf table

with the della Robbia-blue bowl he always wanted.
He drapes a purple velvet swag and arranges

the perfect still life: the bowl, ceramic-potted
cymbidium orchid, red Bohemia vase, ornate tray

from Kashmir overflowing with pears and grapes
as if he knows how soon he will enter a room

blank as a studio backdrop where
the only moveable thing will be an IV stand;

the only art, snow fields shaped from sheets,
shattered ice in a translucent glass.

Brad Is Found

waterlogged

and curled against the bathtub's curved porcelain,
hands clasped between

bloated thighs,
fingertips stained aquatic blue.

He says he has attained transcendence
in the belly of the whale.

Heard the voice of God:

> *Thou shall count every molecule of water,*
> *each whale bone's white gradations,*
> *ripples and the surges;*
>
> *know the drain as worm hole*
> *to the universe, or hell.*
>
> *Time is water.*

Later that night, his day at sea
floats away like sediment,

leaving him safe for a time
on the shoreline of his lover's arms.

His Phone Call

roils the surface of my sleep. I wake
to a voiceless line, hearing
only spasms of expressway traffic,
a scrap of song.

Still, I know it is him,
tongue-tied by terror and shivering
at each wing-sweep of his lungs.

Virused and pain-seared, he lingers
at the intersection
of dying and undying

      (At what point does he drift off to sleep,
      boat becalmed in dreams?),

needing to hear my voice.

Love's umbilical cord, invisible, absolute,
threads air.

Twenty-Four Hours

My son tells me that last week when
Tony ran out of miracles, his family arrived too late

for his mother to touch his hands,
for his father to thumb-close his eyes.

•

The parents who whipped him for playacting in dresses / unchurched him
as incurable sinner / a reparative failure / called him queer.

•

The very next day his father served
notice to vacate the apartment
to Tony's lover

AIDS leper lying in *extremis*

on a soiled mattress in the corner
without hope of resurrection.

•

Then, eyeing possessions like looters,
they bubble-wrapped the crystal vases and a favorite antique *figura*,

fingerprinted linens,
up-turned sofa and chairs in the search for silver.

•

What they didn't take, they doused with gasoline:
    photos of his friends in wet bathing suits poolside in Palm Springs
    faces he wore along Sunset at Halloween, the rhinestone tiara
    gold-plated statuette
    black satin jockstrap
    his last TV script

•

Each of my son's words a deep-throated howl:
Mother, hold me.

The Love of My Son's Life

He says some days you come home from work
with *empanadas, mendocinas,* or *salteñas.*
Some days miraculous toys,
some days an armful of sweet-blooming Stargazer lilies.

Some days you wear Mickey Mouse ears;
another, a tuxedo with swish and tango. You are

whatever Brad wants you to be: his garden,
pool of healing waters, Chippendale stud.

Your love conquers even the vultures
perched on the dresser in the corner of the room.

Every day when you come home and find fever
a crown in his hair, latitudes awry, you serenade him

with Argentinean lullabies and the sweetest of lisps,
sugar his forehead with your fieriest kisses.

The Promise

Last night's killing frost
has flushed the meadow

to still life—

    Mother, I am dying,

fog feathered pines,
bearded grass

    fog filled throat—thrush
    mums the palate
    and now
    a contagion of purple trillium
    spreads across the field
    of my chest

from field's edge
the fox slinks,
gray flag swinging
from its muscled jaws.

Come.

I will, late today, because I know
you are moving
across an unknown field far away.

     My body is
         a broken cup.

Hush, Son, tomorrow we'll cup
our ears,

pretend to hear
the far sounds
of a meadow—the breeze,
the bees.

AIDS Ward, City of Angels, 1995

Even as Brad's thrush-full,
pith-white throat
numbs to water—you

sit on the sweat-stained bed,
cotton swabs in ungloved hands,
pulling viscous strings into a tissue

as if this were no more a chore
than mopping figure eights
along endless corridors.

You brush his teeth and rinse until
the mouth is infant
and ready for your sleight-of-hand trick:

sweet orange removed from
your pocket, peeled and pinwheeled
over the tray table,

each pulpy wafer placed
on his tongue—
you husband him.

Surgical Mask in the Time of Plague

Half my face erased, only eyes
above horizon—unmoored
from a crooked nose,
muffled mouth.

The nurses insist I wear a mask—
white as blisters,
as bone, as mausoleum marble.

Snow fort.

What have other mothers done
in times like these:

Hide in their homes?

Come swaddled
in gown and booties, blue-gloved?

Or do some of them attend, defiant—
faces bare?

For days I have kissed my son
through paper—
sail billowing with each exhale.

Now watching him again turn away
from me as if a stranger,
I choose.

I Find in the Medicine Cabinet

an array of medicine bottles, white
as milkweed silk

and labeled with black box warnings:

shadows are known to bleed into every
room of the body;

sliver of quarter moon will blind.

Juxtapose two incompatible medicines
hours scour
like hawthorn's tangled branches;
alien voices hive inside
the head.

Beware the thrush-caked
tongue thirsting for light
or dark
from the palm-shaped end of a spoon.

In the bathroom—
retrovir and *didanosine* and *lamivudine*—
each with its season of promise.

Years spent wishing for
a miracle drug that would scythe
virus fields barren without
side effects, dominos
cascading into their own toxicity.

Something...heal my son so he can return
to this air.

Hope

Benjamin Button jellyfish, buoyant in the heavy
cadence of crosscurrents, even Death's. I

know its transparent bell, clapper
cruciform-shaped within a circle of alien fingers

searching molecules for good news
even when it is stabbed with despair's fine needle.

Look at how it shapeshifts, tucking inward and

crumpling to elemental gristle until
it is larval and anchored

to the body's declensions,
each unpredictable change in mercurial degrees

then resurrects from the cellular crucible—

glistening rush to spawn polyps, which
plump and lengthen,

bud anew. Leaving me to believe for another day
in the way it ripples

through ribbons of light. Shimmers.

Hospital Waltz

Alone, except for bougainvillea
feverish with color and

two giant palms,
we stumble, step by impossible step,

in a waltz around the flagstone patio,
past his wheelchair, sundial

casting its late shadow.
Mother and child, pulse to pulse,

moving to notes only he hears,
breathing together

as when I was full with him
before his heels pushed him free.

How can he dance?

Only as one drawn to life's joys,
prodigal moth to pure light.

My Son Confesses

Each night you lower
the bed rail behind the white wings

of curtains and crawl in beside him, defiant
of sheets that are blood-smudged,

spongy with sweat, sour with fluids.

Brushing away tendrils of tubes,
trace the labyrinths of his body—

first with your fingertips and then
lips over tissue-thin skin.

He knows it is love that defies
as you, monitoring the vital signs—

offered groin, rising heat, racehorse pulse—
ride his white-knuckled shudders

over the edge to a place beyond pain.

MADELYN GARNER

Sunday Afternoon Visiting Hours

In the garden, lilacs
bloom

from the under-
story
of leaves. Under

his eyes
bone rims thumb-sized
shadows.

He shifts in bed,
whispers,

the lilacs
seem softer
this year.

I touch the back
of his hand
at the place of blood-

knots.The sun
descends beyond
the threshold,

shades of bruise
spread.

A vase overflows.

His dying
lilacs the room.

What I Didn't Know

The way the mind, casting for loaves and fishes, snags his broken boots, nautilus on a sill, a name repeating. Unpredictable as Santa Ana winds or the way a rotted stair trembles underfoot. Chronic as mosquitoes. Constant as night. Days groping without a lamp or rope in total blueness. Tongue reduced to the words: *infinite loop, vortex, black hole.* And pain—flesh sizzling from the lightest touch. Bludgeoned. No cup of tea to quench mourning's terrible thirst. What laughter? What joy? He is unmendable.

What the Body Knows

All night he waits for family
and the drawing back
of the blackout curtains to fill him
with sunlight and hope.

Daily, we bear a copper bowl brimful
with hot water, finest triple-milled soap,
sponge and a thick white towel.

Hands heavy with oils
we massage his back in a rhythm constant
as tides, count the abacus beads
of his spine

and circle the calves with wobbly O's,
pull his perfect toes until
his breath matches
the hushed exhalation
of eucalyptus leaves outside.

Then we lay our hands on his body,
such a small boat, clasping it firmly
to the shore of the living.

Triptych: His Final Days

As Treacherous Bed

Because his back hisses each time he is pulled
across grit-rough sheets,

I must lift my son to check his body, finding
not pock or red splotch that blanches

under fingertip, but blood that leaks
from wounds I cannot bear to touch. The way

I ache for the child I rocked:
his infant skin, warm and fragrant,

peach soft in my arms—
body incandescent as sunlit milk.

Hard to believe this skin splitting in increments
along the spine—reminder of how prone

we are to rot. Soon the room
is filled with the smell of decay

too far gone for succor: alchemy, debridement,
the useless flaying by surgical knife.

As Intravenous Feeding

He no longer strokes his boyfriend's hair or
the rose petals languishing on his nightstand.

No matter how thirsty, he must wait
for my hand to pick up a water glass.

In the brain a trillion neurons, low voltage and erratic,
refuse to send messages to limbs turned phantom:

pick up the spoon.

There is no morsel sweet enough for his hands
to find a way to bring it to his mouth.

As Morphine Drip

He refuses drugs even though
what is left of him could rise untethered

toward the ceiling,
swaddled in ether, in oblivion,

circling over a landscape narrowing to skeletal.
Candle flickering in a paper lantern.

As though he knows morphine-weighted
eyelids will never again open,

for days he stays awake even as his body
grows cold as milk; the pain he welcomes.

For Days He Has Been Quiet as Bone

so when his eyes flick open it   knocks us out   this jack-in-the-box   words forming
a new path to a clear question: have you watered my orchids?   O he is handsome
he is laughing   holds our hands   hope appears gift-wrapped with silver ribbons
we sit on his bed as we lap   at the past like feral cats   whoop and laugh   make
streamers of stories   party balloons bounce against the ceiling   until the room
softens at its corners   at dawn he falls asleep   never comes back.

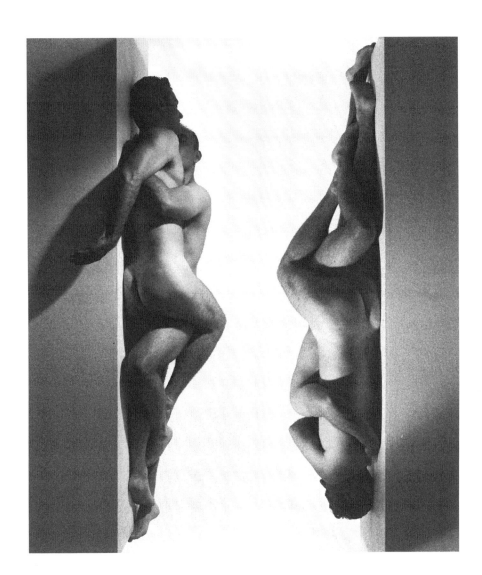

The Law of Probability

If it were a late-spring day,
I might count sparrows
converging on the backyard's cable lines

(the same one or is it two?),
might graph wing flicks
or their song.

Discover the prime numbers of squirrels
storing hawthorn berries
(qualitatively more red than usual),

theories of randomness derived from
their frenetic motions
rearranging holes.

The number
of flax seeds in the morning toast,
molecules in a glass of water,
tea leaves.

This drifting sift of flour—how many ounces
of ash does it equal? And with what
exactitude can any of it be

measured? His body
or grief's weight, doubling for how long,
and at what rate?

Arrow of Time

In alternate universes planets kiss
and time jitters
like a grasshopper in eleven dimensions,
swarms backward—
wasp to a state of eggdom.

Here, where Earth circles
the Sun in one direction, time
is a new tulip bed behind
the kitchen, a shovel's friction

loosening the clay, sprinkle
of blood meal for the Red Emperors
you did not live to see
lifting their heads

in petal harmonics to April rain.
Please. Stand again at the dark edge
of the porch. The season before you heard
the first intercellular explosion,
collapse of galaxies.

In This Photograph

His eyes veiled, body a candle
       devoured by its own fire
to wick and smolder
is not how I remember

the archived hands, paint-splattered,
moving across a canvas. Where
is the sunlight as if some
angel restored the livid places to white?
Where hair once the color of graphite,
       and curly?

There is nothing that shows
him whole—
       this figure made of light
as in *lumen*—

and I am betrayed
       not by cone and rod,
but everything I thought I knew
about dying could be
otherwise.

Redshift

Last night in my dreams,
I find him
among synapses sparkling like
Dorothy's slippers;

his red kite rising, turning back
on itself as Möbius strip
above Carmel's shore-line spray. How
many years ago—
thirty-five or is it forty?

There he is with his Red Flyer Wagon.

A split lip from falling.

Standing before a bed of crimson tulips—
a favorite color.

His first velvet jacket, scarlet
like stained glass at dusk.

Plasma beads on the back of his hand.

His first breath: stunned blue eyes
staring into the space
between us: we shift red.

Schrödinger's Cat

Today as the sun stitches
the screen door into a needlepoint of light,
the cat, a shadow on the threshold,
is oblivious to the squirrels
scurrying along the vertebrae of a fence.
Stilled slink. Only a twitch
of ear proving, for this click of time,
she is alive.

I consider the possibility
of a parallel universe where an identical cat,
defenseless against the slaughter
of wheels, drags home viscera
shiny as beetles and dies
stretched before the threshold,
breeze fraying her fur.

That is to say, time is a roundelay
in the quantum garden
of many worlds, our paths crossing
and separating in alternate
realities cloned from the same streaming
particles, bursts of energy.
My mind says *Yes*
to infinite copies of him coming
to the door, young
and transcendent with good blood,
bearing a kitten the color of shadows

Spring Lament

The garden is sullen,
its green resurrection matted down
under bark shards and branches
and maple leaves dry as snakeskin.
The pear tree's buds are tight
sailors' knots. Even the tulips, stunned
by yesterday's cold winds,
refuse to liberate their blades
from the raw ground.

The *Farmer's Almanac* insists
that spring will arrive with its sprays
of forsythia to be cut and arranged
into yellow metaphor,
but the only flowers on my table
are plastic.

Earth, are you conspiring against me?

My womb, old empty pot, cannot replace
what it has lost, but I am ready to nurture
seedlings, tack clematis to trellis,
chase off aphid and beetles.

If only you will tilt.

Enough

I wake this morning thinking of a son cut off
        at mid-blossom,
but dawn's garden is insistent:

Come, the plum trees are fruiting—
        violet-green pendants swelling toward sweetness—

hummingbirds spangle in earth's early light.

Even the saw-toothed sunflowers are ticking their way toward multiplying.

I stand knee-deep among
ox-eye, star-studded yarrow, prairie coneflower in this place where

the grass from yesterday's rain-drench
presses against the gate of my head for a way in—

to smooth out grief, cover it,
bury it under.

From the Beginning

Scientists studied epidemic clusters
for the scratch that started the AIDS conflagration:

harrowing speed
by which viral mutations multiplied

until a single kiss evicted
loved ones from their bodies.

•

Driven, they puzzled threads
across maps,

red zigzags

tracking everyone in the Cameroons
who ever dreamt in simian,

rumors of the plague as deadly cargo
stored aboard lonely workers

returning home from the edges
of the world.

•

One crucial report: the Haitian nurse
and his behaviors—

unaware he would add
this misery to all the others

on his green-shrouded island
before he died.

•

And what to make of the flight attendant
suggested as Patient Zero?

The one who played doctor in the dark.

Look, he said afterward,
clicking on a hall light

to show sarcoma's purple fingerprints
on his pretty neck.

•

They followed blood samples across
apocalyptic landscapes,

carved cadavers,
replicated conditions—

all those shooting stars in a universe of billions—
taking no notice of one son lost in a plague of coordinates.

But to me: *patient Alpha / patient Omega.*

Acknowledgments

The author wishes to thank the journals or presses in which these poems appeared, some in other forms.

Calyx: "Spring Lament" and "The Last Birthday Gift"

Florida Review: "Camera Obscura" and "I Find in the Medicine Cabinet"

Georgetown Review: "Ash"

Harpur Palate: "Schrödinger's Cat"

HeartLodge: "What the Body Knows"

HIV, Here & Now (online): "The Love of My Son's Life," "My Son Confesses," and "AIDS Ward, City of Angels, 1995"

Nimrod International Journal: "Enough" and "Surgical Mask in the Time of Plague"

Slant: "Body Studies in Black and White"

So to Speak (online): "My Son Confesses"

Tiger's Eye: "Elegy for Memory"

Water-Stone Review: "Arrow of Time," "AIDS Ward, City of Angels, 1995," "When He Tells," "The Years Between," and "For Days He Has Been Quiet as Bone"

"The Phone Call" appeared in *Love Over 60: 100 Women Poets Over 60* (Mayapple Press).

"After Braverman's Suicide Suite, Gallery Show, Los Angeles, 1994" was chosen as a finalist in The Robinson Jeffers Tor House 2011 Prize for Poetry.

"Schrödinger's Cat" was chosen as a finalist for The Milton Kessler Memorial Prize for Poetry, *Harpur Palate*, 2007.

"What the Body Knows" appeared in the 2012 *Women Artists Datebook* (Syracuse Cultural Workers).

In Appreciation

I would like to thank the many writers and colleagues at Lighthouse Writers Workshop who supported me while writing this book, too numerous to list by name. A special note of gratitude to Michael Burwell, Lise Goett, Veronica Golos, Joseph Hutchison, Kimberly Johnson, Laurie Kutchins, Sheryl Luna, Kate Northrop, Seth Brady Tucker, and Leslie Ullman for their valuable insights and guidance. Thank you to Andrea Watson, editor extraordinaire at 3: A Taos Press, and Jeffrey Levine, at Tupelo Press, for the selection of my manuscript in the Tupelo Press July Open Reading 2015. Finally, my love and thanks to my family: daughters, Michele Braverman and Alicia LaPiano, who continually sustain me; sons-in-law, Russell LaPiano and Tomislav Beslic; grandchildren, Desanka, Grey, and Rowan; sister, Judith Tuffield, and brother, Gerald Garner; my son's special dear ones, Omar Pugach and Lisa Liermann; and my son, Bradley Joseph Braverman, who is dearly missed.

About The Author

Master teacher, editor, and poet, Madelyn Garner has degrees from the University of Denver and Mills College. As a creative writing instructor, middle school principal, and mentor, she is widely recognized for designing and implementing a variety of innovative educational programs at all levels, elementary through university. Among her educational achievements and honors, she is the recipient of the Colorado Governor's Award for Excellence in the Arts and Humanities for encouraging incorporation of the arts into school programs and her leadership in providing students multiple opportunities in the field of writing.

Named a Leo Love Merit Scholar at the Taos Summer Writers' Conference, Madelyn also was awarded an Aspen Writers' Foundation's Annual Writing Retreat Scholarship. In 2010, she won the Jackson Hole Writers Conference Poetry Prize. As co-editor, she edited and published the anthology, *Collecting Life: Poets on Objects Known and Imagined*, in 2011. Over the years, Madelyn has been a featured poet at numerous readings as well as collaborative *ekphrasis* events held throughout the United States. Recent work has appeared in *The Best American Poetry*, 2015, *The Florida Review, The Pinch, Slant, Roanoke Review, Nimrod International Journal, The Journal of Feminist Studies in Religion*, and *Water-Stone Review*, among others.

She lives in Denver, Colorado, along with her daughters and grandchildren.

About The Artist

Bradley Braverman studied graphic design, print-making, and painting at the Kansas City Art Institute; the Saci Studio Art Center in Florence, Italy; and Amherst College. After a brief period as a free-lance artist in New York, Braverman moved to Los Angeles where he worked in the studio of L A fashion designer Choey Fang as well as art director for both Matt Sterling and Associated Video group. Eventually, he set up shop as a graphic designer, with design work appearing in national publications and his fine art represented by galleries from Los Angeles to New York. Braverman's commercial work was recognized by the 1992 PDN/ Nikon Award for Excellence. His other interests included the production of art films which invited comparisons with Robert Mapplethorpe. His last gallery show, in September 1995 at the Grand Arts, Kansas City, Missouri, featured both a billboard-sized photo series and a sampling of his early black-and-white formal work. The artist died in January 1996 at the age of 34 of AIDS.

Also By 3: A Taos Press

Collecting Life: Poets on Objects Known and Imagined
Madelyn Garner and Andrea Watson

Seven
Sheryl Luna

The Luminosity
Bonnie Rose Marcus

Trembling in the Bones: A Commemorative Edition
Eleanor Swanson

3 A.M.
Phyllis Hotch

Ears of Corn: Listen
Max Early

Elemental
Bill Brown

Rootwork
Veronica Golos

Farolito
Karen S. Córdova

Godwit
Eva Hooker

The Ledgerbook
William S. Barnes

The Mistress
Catherine Strisik

Library of Small Happiness
Leslie Ullman

Day of Clean Brightness
Jane Lin

Bloodline
Radha Marcum